Barns of America

Barns of America

Author
Bill Harris

Photography
Jerry Irwin

CLB 2157
© 1991 Colour Library Books Ltd, Godalming, Surrey, England.
All rights reserved.
This 1991 edition published by Crescent Books,
distributed by Outlet Book Company, Inc, a Random House Company,
225 Park Avenue South, New York, New York 10003.
Color reproduction by Advance Laser Graphic Arts Ltd, Hong Kong.
Printed and bound in Hong Kong.
ISBN 0 517 05312 8
8 7 6 5 4 3 2 1

**CRESCENT BOOKS
NEW YORK**

A flower farm, Mount Vernon, Washington.

When American architects began establishing themselves as an influence independent of the old traditions, one of their first dictates was that "form follows function." Before long, they followed that with another rule, that said in good design, "less is more."

Probably not many farmers in America were regular readers of *Architectural Record* or any of the other publications that kept the world in touch with what seemed to be an aesthetic revolution at the turn of the century. But if any of them were aware of the innovations that were changing the face of cities like Chicago and New York, they probably couldn't help smiling. Every American farmer had a perfect example of the newly discovered ideals within an easy walk of the kitchen door.

A stone barn, Farragut, Pennsylvania.

And no architect had anything to do with it. Tradition, on the other hand, had everything to do with it.

The form of the typical American barn begins with a tradition that was already old when the ancient Egyptians separated wheat and other grains from their husks by beating them on dirt floors with whip-like tools called flails. Over the centuries, barn-like structures were developed to enclose the threshing floors, and to make a tough job easier, storage areas called mows were built into the sidewalls to stack the unthreshed sheaves and to hold the threshed grain until a windy day, when it could be tossed into the air to allow the wind to carry off the lighter chaff in a process called winnowing. By the mid-eighteenth century, when American farmers were adapting European ideas to their own special needs, much of the threshing was already being done by machine, but the big open space in the center of their barns was at the heart of every plan.

The first European barns enclosed much more than just a threshing floor, of course, and the Americans followed their ancestors' example to incorporate other features, too. But there was one very important exception. The American barn was intended to be a workplace, rarely a living space. In Europe, farmers had combined the barn, which was originally developed for the storage of grain, with the byre, a place for housing animals, and their own house. The pattern had changed in many places by the seventeenth century, when farmers began leaving for America, but it was still followed in Central and Eastern Europe, which would contribute more to the basic American design than any other culture. In nearly every case, the

East Albany barns, Vermont.

Once the pride of a farm in Potlatch, Idaho, an old barn shelters little more than memories now, a victim of the same sun and rain that make the surrounding wheat fields so productive.

Old World barn was a long, rectangular building with a central threshold, but it also included galleries for cows and horses, and at one end a fireplace provided heat for comfort and for cooking. The open threshing floor was the living room, furnished with chairs and tables that provided a little comfort, though precious little, at the end of a busy day. Family members and hired hands slept in galleries over the animals. For reasons lost to history, it was traditional for women to sleep over the cows and the men upstairs above the horses. Pigs, mercifully, were kept in a separate space at the opposite end of the structure, and the space above them was used for fodder storage. Eventually, but probably not a moment too soon,

someone had the bright idea to separate the living quarters from the rest of the structure, and the end with the fireplace was divided into rooms. But animals and people still shared the same roof, as they had for centuries.

History is also rather silent on how they coped with smells under those thatched roofs. When early American farmers began living in their barns, they apparently didn't consider that a problem. But summers tend to be hotter in North America than in Europe, and after a season or two of heat and humidity they began to think about making other arrangements. But what finally pushed them out of their barns was not the heat of summer. It was cold winters that did the trick. In the traditional European

The barns and other outbuildings of a Pennsylvanian dairy farm should extend their well-ordered usefulness far into the future.

12

barns, a peat fire burned constantly, not only to take the chill off the living quarters and to warm the farmer's food but the smoke, which escaped through a hole in the roof, also cured the meat that was hanging from the rafters. In America where there was an unlimited supply of wood, but not as much peat, the fires were not only smokier but much more dangerous in a place where hay and straw were stored. It wasn't long before the American tradition dictated that a farm should have not one, but a collection of buildings that included smoke houses, ice houses, spring houses and, of course, a separate house for the farmer and his family. But most important of all was the barn. In the early days of American settlement it was the only building worthy of the name constructed after the land was cleared, and the owners usually waited until seven or eight harvests were in before they turned their attention to the farmhouse, living in the meantime in a cabin they had thrown together when they first began cutting the clearing that would become their farm.

Architectural historians are usually silent on the subject of barns, but those who have studied them are almost always impressed by the way they resemble churches, and some even feel that when Europeans began building houses of worship, their inspiration came from the barns around them. It's a chicken-and-egg discussion that will probably never be resolved. But the classic description of the American barn is "basilic," a term the early Christians borrowed from the Romans, who built basilicas as great halls where the citizens could mingle with royalty. As a church, the basilica followed a plan with an open

A Victorian treasure in the Maryland hills.

15

A Chevvy pickup, Oaksdale, Washington.

central area and side aisles covered with a timber roof. In other words, a barn.

The Christian basilicas also included a tower, and the comparison might be extended to liken the silo to it. But those towers didn't appear on barns until after the American Civil War, when a farmer in Indiana built a tall wooden cylinder to store his fodder. The idea travelled to other parts of the country, but it was a slow process and the first above-ground silos didn't begin appearing east of the Appalachians until the 1890s. Before that, corn and potatoes and feed for livestock were stored underground in silos adapted from the weatherproof pits the Indians had developed. As the idea of above-ground storage began taking hold, it was obvious that many farmers didn't have their heart in it. Most of their silos were just boards standing upright and held together with hoops, which is why only a few of the early examples still exist, and those that do are often leaning at drunken angles. When the idea reached New England, in

fact, they built them inside the barn and made them square. It didn't take them long to find out that the shape was wrong, usually discovering the error of their ways the first time they had to clean it out. Beyond that, having it inside allowed the wood to dry out and shrink, and before long air began getting at their silage and spoiling it. Before too many seasons went by all of the silos were moved outdoors and every one of them was round. By then, particularly in the Northeast, the supply of wood, which had once been so great it was almost considered a nuisance, was considerably reduced and it was cheaper to build the new silos of stone, which helps explain why after a century there are so many silos still standing without a barn attached to them.

The original stone silos, which began appearing on dairy farms in Michigan and Wisconsin in the 1880s, still followed the old tradition, with most of their storage space below ground. Most of them went deeper into the

Classic symmetry, Monroe City, Ohio.

ground that they rose above it, and their cylindrical towers extended not much higher than the roof line of the barn. Eventually, practicality led to taller cylinders, where it was easier to get the stored material out. The stone walls were often as much as three feet thick, which insures that they'll be a part of the landscape for a long time to come. The same, unfortunately, can't be said for many of the barns that were the pride and joy of earlier generations of Americans.

The first American adaptation of European designs came to us from Holland by way of the Hudson River Valley and other Dutch settlements between the Hudson and Delaware Rivers. Though the style has evolved into something purely American since the seventeenth century, it is still known as the Dutch barn, characterized by large doors at each end rather than along the sides. That was an innovation of the practical Dutch, who found it simpler to drive their wagons through the barn from one end to the other without bothering to turn them around. The doors also provided a cross draft at threshing time and made it easier to keep the barn clean, a matter of some importance to a Dutch farmer.

In another bow to cleanliness, the Dutch introduced the idea of raising the central threshing floor above the stalls where cattle and horses were kept. It was a good arrangement for keeping the stables and pens clean, but it also made feeding easier because the livestock faced inward and was supplied with food from the raised floor in the middle without having to lift it. It was an innovation made simpler in America, where the abundance of wood made it possible to build the floors of thick planks rather than having to dig trenches in the

A Montana blockhouse.

hard-packed dirt that had been the method used back home.

The early barns of New England followed a much different pattern. The English had developed a simple plan that included a threshing floor and two mows, and other Europeans had followed their lead long before anyone thought of settling in North America. Naturally, transplanted English farmers followed the pattern their fathers had found practical, but the English barn also came to America in the heads of immigrants from other countries. The Yankees improved on the design almost immediately, partly because farming in America wasn't quite the same, but mostly because of the availability of wood in almost unbelievable quantities. Because they were able to cut beams of larger sizes, the American farmers were able to extend the threshing floor and build a loft above it for the storage of fodder. A single thick beam as much as sixty feet long supported the floor and the loft above it as well as forming part of the truss that carried the entire weight of the building, even when it was filled to capacity and had a load of snow on the roof. The Americans also departed from Old World tradition by building entirely of wood, rather than of brick or stone, as they would have done back home in England.

The basic English barn didn't include space for animals, but the early American farmers, most of whom concentrated on grain production, didn't have much need for it, and what livestock they had could easily be housed by slightly modifying the design. In the mid-nineteenth century, when the emphasis shifted to animal husbandry, farmers met the challenge by expanding their barns to include a byre. Sometimes

Sheltering wings, Cheney, Pennsylvania.

the building was simply extended out from one end, but most of the time it seemed more practical to build a wing at right angles to the original structure to form a sheltered yard. As time went on, many farmers built a second wing at right angles to the first to form an area enclosed on three sides, and sometimes even a third ell to create a courtyard.

The first barns Englishmen built in America had thatched roofs just like the ones they remembered back home. But it didn't take them long to find out that thatch tends to rot in the North American climate, and they quickly changed to slate or cedar shingles. But in the process, they didn't bother to change the pitch of the roof which, even on new barns, remained steep as if to accommodate thatch for a further century-and-a-half. Except for the fact that a forty-five degree roof sheds snow more easily, no one knows why the Yankee farmers didn't take advantage of the opportunity to get the extra space a gentler slope would give them. But, curiously, when the winds of war began blowing in the 1760s, people who were loyal to the Mother Country demonstrated their loyalty by raising the pitch of their barn roofs, reflecting a change that had been made back in England a century earlier.

Most of the earliest American barns were built by the farmers themselves, relying on lessons handed down from father to son. But before long, manuals that had served carpenters in good stead in the building and decoration of houses began to address themselves to the art of barn-building as well. One of the earliest of them began by cautioning that strength and convenience were the two most essential qualities to take into account, but warned its readers not to get carried away. "Fanciful ornaments are frequently introduced with no better

A Kentucky tobacco barn.

Brick and stone silos frequently outlast the wooden barns they serve. But in this case, on a farm in New York State, there still seems to be plenty of life left in both.

This Iowa barn is known as a hog sales pavilion.

intention than to disguise blemishes in proportion and symmetry," it said. "The due proportion of correspondence of parts constitute a beauty that always first attracts the eye; and where beauty is wanting carving and gilding only excite disgust. In like manner, the affectation of gaudy dress in a man who has the misfortune to be deformed answers no other purpose than to invite ridicule." Or, as the style-setters of the early 20th century would have put it, "less is more."

American farmers hardly needed to be reminded of such things. Most of them didn't even bother to paint their barns, and the beams that held them up were always left in their rough cut stage with no other attempt at decoration than the owner's name or initials and possibly a date. But the exception in the early years of the American colonies came from the Puritans of New England, who, although they equated plainness with Godliness in just about everything, were among the first to paint their barns and the first to add decorative cupolas to their roofs. The latter sometimes provided ventilation, but were more important for attracting pigeons, which provided most farm families with food as well as oil for their lamps.

When the early builders began covering their roofs with pine shingles, the wood strips were traditionally laid on raw, and though the farmers were careful to remove any trees that might shade the barn but cause dry rot in the process, they usually tried to leave at least one tall pine tree standing. They knew that the tree would shed its needles onto the roof and that was exactly what they wanted it to do. They knew that the pine needles would encourage moss to grow, and the combination would create an insulating blanket. It also preserved the wood and helped make it watertight, not to mention adding a look of natural beauty that has survived in many barns after a century of all kinds of weather. There is a scientific principle involved, to be sure, but the barn builders gave themselves an edge with a bit of folk science dictating that the only way to make certain that the pine-moss blanket would form properly was to construct their roofs only during nights of the new moon. Some others hedged their bets by heating the shingles before nailing them in place, and some even smeared them with cow manure in hopes they'd last longer. But, as the test of time has proven, the wood alone had lasting qualities even if nothing was done to it and it was hammered into place in broad daylight! In fact, in some parts of New England there are examples of roofs whose nails have long since rusted away but are still watertight and seem qualified to keep on doing their job for another hundred years. Of course, they may be the ones that were put there by the light of the new moon!

The idea of painting the wood in either houses or barns didn't come along until just before the Revolutionary War, but once it did Americans began painting everything in sight, even outdoor privies. The idea took hold in Virginia first, where they added lampblack to turpentine and linseed oil to create a light gray paint that not only soaked into the wood as a preservative, but gave a pleasing light gray accent of color to the man-made landscape. It wasn't long before they were adding iron oxide and clay to produce reds and orange-yellows that gave an even more pleasing look to their barns and other outbuildings. Up north, where natural colors and oils weren't as plentiful, but the desire to gussy-up the

Ready for the harvest in La Conner, Washington.

place was just as strong, farmers discovered that if they added iron oxide, common rust which they had in abundance, to skimmed milk and lime and a bit of linseed oil, it made a tough, enamel-like paint that didn't soak into the wood like the stuff the Southerners were using. It dried quickly to form a hard shell and, as history has proven, it usually lasted for decades before another coat had to be applied. The only problem, if it can be called a problem, was that it came in just one color, red. The result was that nearly every barn in the northeast was painted red by the beginning of the eighteenth century, and it's still the color of choice nearly two hundred years later.

Naturally, there were hundreds of farmers who still didn't paint their barns at all in spite of the new fashion. It went beyond their inclination to let nature take its course. More often than not it was a kind of prejudice against the Germans who were moving into Pennsylvania and were not only painting their barns, but adding colorful decorations they called "hex signs," which outsiders were convinced were put there to scare the devil away. New Englanders who often blamed their hard luck on witches thought that such affectations smacked of paganism and even believed that painting a barn red was an expression of some kind of vague superstition. They considered themselves much too sophisticated for such things. In their culture it was much better to burn witches than to simply frighten them away. And since red was the only color available to them, they decided that natural wood was symbolic of Godliness. Besides, in most cases paint was just an affectation, anyway. Most of the early barns were sided and roofed

Louvers in Gettysburg, Pennsylvania.

One of the lasting glories of Rome, Georgia.

with shingles that breathed with changes in the atmosphere and contracted when they were wet. It was a perfect answer to the problem of making a building airtight when it rained but allowed air to pass through when it was dry. One of the delights of being inside a barn on a sunny summer day is the pattern of light created by holes in the walls and the roof. Your first reaction is that the place must be in need of repair and won't offer much protection on a rainy day. But when the humidity rises the shingles will come together and plug the holes. If they were painted that wouldn't happen. On the other hand, if they were painted, the chinks wouldn't appear, either.

The Germans and Swiss in Pennsylvania usually denied that the geometric patterns they used to decorate their barns had any significance beyond simple beauty. When pressed, the farmers usually said that the signs were inspired by the designs on the quilts their wives made. But they never gave

An 1835 New York farm and its 1914 barn.

any hint that they, too, were originally intended to ward off witches and other evil spirits. Their denials were only natural. It's obviously never a good idea to reveal your secret strategy in the struggle against the forces of evil. Besides, every farmer knew that all the defense that was required against witches was to hang a worn horseshoe over the door. Witches, as everyone knew, had an uncontrollable curiosity as well as a fascination for mathematics. Any witch about to enter a door who saw an inverted horseshoe there would be forced by her natural bent to stop and figure out how many hoofprints the shoe had made. The older and more worn the shoe, the better it worked, because it would have made so many prints it would take the witch an entire night to count them. At dawn she would have to flee, and if she came back another night she would have to start counting all over again. Some farmers confounded witches even more by putting piles of grain outside the door, knowing that no self-respecting witch could pass it by without counting every grain. Better still, they sometimes ground the corn into meal to make the counting more of a time-consuming challenge. With weapons like these, any Pennsylvania Dutch farmer will tell you that painting symbols on barn sides to confound witches was surely redundant, and assure you that the designs are there for no better reason than "for pretty."

The Pennsylvania Dutch also decorated their barns with representations of animals as well as their own names and an occasional inspirational message. But the idea didn't travel well to other parts of America until the early part of this century, when travelling salesmen toured the countryside offering to paint barns in return for the right to use one side to paint an advertising message aimed at people who were beginning to take to the road in their new automobiles. Like the cars that came in a choice of any color as long as it was black, the itinerant barn-painters preferred the traditional red, which went better with things like Coca-Cola and Mail Pouch Tobacco.

But if America's farmers were slow to accept the Pennsylvanians' penchant for color in their outbuildings, they had to admit that the Pennsylvania barn was a joy to behold, even before it was painted. The basic design has its origins in Switzerland, and came to America by way of Germany in the minds of Mennonite farmers, whose fathers and grandfathers had been forced out of their original homes in the Swiss Alps and resettled in the Black Forest of Germany. Their original homesteads, which combined living quarters for the farmer's family and his livestock under a common roof, were built into hillsides. The section

Cheerful contrasts to the Washington winter.

for human habitation was a two-story affair attached to, but separate from, the barn area, which had stalls for cattle and horses at grade level, entered through doors in the side. The lowest level was usually built of stone, but the floors above it, which included the threshing floor and the hayloft, were faced with logs. The upper floor was reached from the hill behind through wide doors at the opposite end of the structure from the living quarters, an innovation that nicely separated the living and working environment. It was a giant step in the direction of the creation of the separate farmhouse. The entire structure could be as much as one hundred feet long, but seen from the front it appeared to be a compact house, usually with an overhanging second floor creating a sheltered porch so that some of the kitchen chores could be done outdoors in nice weather.

When the Germans arrived in America they modified the design, first of all by building a separate farmhouse, a simple step that made it possible completely to revolutionize the barns of their fathers. They still kept the livestock at grade level and put the threshing floor and mows above them. And they also brought along the idea of the cantilevered extension of the second floor, which not only gave them extra storage space inside, but provided an overhang that protected the doors and windows on the first level. The Americanized version was also usually built into a hillside, but on this side of the Atlantic its longer side was placed parallel to the hill rather than as had been traditional in the Old Country. The innovation allowed for a longer gallery under the second floor at the front of the barn, which was perfect for sheltering cattle on cold, windy days. It

This barn in Gettysburg, Pennsylvania, gives shelter to livestock.

was a creature comfort not available in the European version, where the space in front was more often filled with geraniums and other flowers, and animals were never welcome.

The second floor was still designated as a threshing floor, but in most of the American barns still standing, the space is now called the drive floor because it is used for unloading wagons of wheat and hay and for winter storage of the farm machinery. In the Pennsylvania barn it is reached through tall doors that open directly on the crest of the hill, and if there was no hill high enough the farmer banked earth against the north side of the barn, no easy job in those days before bulldozers were invented.

The south-facing front wall of the Pennsylvania barn is always of wood to allow for the cantilevered overhang, but sometimes the other walls, especially the gable ends, which usually faced the windier east and west sides, were built of brick or stone. Like the Dutch barns and the English barns in nearby colonies, they are all basically of wood frame construction, but the German barn-builders had an idea that the only wood worth using was oak, with the result that their work has outlasted the efforts of their contemporaries even though, in the opinion of modern farmers, it may have outlived its original usefulness.

The practical ideas of the Pennsylvanians influenced barn construction in most of the other colonies, but when the country began moving west the model didn't always fit the territory. Many farmers crossed the Alleghenies with the idea of starting over with a prosperous-looking Pennsylvania barn and many actually built them. But most of them missed the

Pennsylvania hillsides often dictate a barn's shape, such as that of this one in Kinzer.

The Amish in Holmes County, Ohio, still raise their barns the old-fashioned way, with everybody in the community helping. Nowadays, though, the beams, siding and window frames are more likely to have come from a lumberyard than to have been handmade.

point. They had the impression that what made the German barn better was that it was bigger, and ignored most of its other qualities. They weren't always too concerned with careful craftsmanship, either, and didn't usually bother to season the wood properly, even neglecting to remove the bark in many cases. And if their barns were big enough to make an impression of prosperity, it wasn't a lasting impression. They were anything but permanent. Then, when they got beyond the Mississippi, even making them bigger wasn't possible.

Once the pioneers were out on the plains they had to cope with different problems and learn new methods of farming. There was no wood to spare for

building barns and they sheltered their sheep and cattle in lean-tos made of sticks and covered with straw that also provided feed for the animals. The barns they did build were as massive as they could raise in the face of the shortage of wood, but they were as simple as the barns put up by the first Europeans in America. But for all that, they became landmarks in the flat countryside, a sign that civilization could take root and even prosper out on the prairie.

Meanwhile, back East farmers were experimenting with new and better designs and in 1826 the Shaker community at Hancock, Massachusetts, came up with a revolutionary idea that seemed to be the model of efficiency. As

they described it, with their design, "a great number of workers might be simultaneously engaged at their tasks and no person be in another's way." It was different in another way, too. The Shaker barn was round.

Over the next half century hundreds of round barns were built in every part of the country, especially in the West, where the shape was perceived as the ideal dairy barn. In many instances, the shape was modified into an octagon, which was easier to build, but the idea was always the same: it included a larger-than-average open floor with a minimum of supporting beams which made storing and handling hay much easier; and it required less material to

build. And because there were no corners, it was easier to keep clean. Better still, many a farmer believed it was a good idea not to have any corners where the devil might hide. But for all the imitations and the opportunities they presented for improving the basic idea, the best example of the art is still the Shaker barn at Hancock, which was rebuilt in 1865 and still stands as an American architectural landmark. Its 36-inch stone walls are 21 feet high and 270 feet around and there is room inside for 52 head of cattle surrounding a hay storage area 55 feet in diameter. And there was plenty of room left over for plenty of people to get on with their work without bumping into each other.

The Plain people of Pennsylvania are well-known for their rejection of the trappings of modern life; visiting their farms is often like taking a trip into a world most of us have long since abandoned.

Hay was loaded from a second-floor wagon area and fed by gravity to the floor below. The roof is supported by a cluster of posts and trusses adapted from the ones developed for windmills, clearly a triumph of engineering light years removed from the simple, but solidly based, construction methods of earlier American barns. But with very few exceptions, the round barn, in spite of all of its advantages, wasn't practical for one of the most fascinating of all the American traditions, the barn-raising. Because round barns usually had to be built by professionals, their cost was beyond the means of most family farms. From the earliest days in America a farmer did most of the work of barn-building himself, and when he needed help there was never a need to pay for it. He invited in the neighbors for a day of fun and incredibly hard work.

They called them "bees," and though every farm community in America was built on the principle of neighbors helping each other when help was needed, the most enthusiastic barn-raisers were the Mennonites in Pennsylvania. Their barns were much bigger than in other places and more people were required to raise them, but even a small structure would get a big turnout. Nobody loved a bee like the Plain People, and more than a quilting bee or a husking bee, they loved a barn-raising bee most of all. Ordinarily, they denied themselves the idea of a party for any occasion, but if a gathering was centered around worship or work, they could become the most eager of all party animals.

By the time the day arrived for the get-together a great deal of work had already been done. Women had been gathering in each other's kitchens for weeks to make sure that no one would

A New Jersey horse farm.

go hungry on the Great Day. They prepared smoked hams and sausages, cooked vegetables, made pickles and sauces, kneaded bread and rolled out endless numbers of pie crusts; and they produced huge crocks of stew big enough to feed an army. The men who would constitute that army, meanwhile, were donating their labor after their own chores were done. The foundation came first. Its walls were up to two feet thick, made of stone and usually without mortar. A heavy wooden beam that would support the structure came next and on top of it sills extended across the top of the foundation to support the floor joists. Flooring went down next, but it wasn't nailed in place. Sometimes nails were hammered in a year or so later, but more often than not the floor was left loose for the life of the barn. While that part of the job was being done, neighbors were at work helping to put the main frame together in sections they called "bents," connecting the members with wooden pegs driven home with a 40-pound wooden hammer known as a "beetle." Each section was numbered with Roman numerals, the kind that could most easily be cut with a chisel, so that when the time came to raise them into place there would be a minimum of confusion. Many years later, the home-building industry came up with the revolutionary idea of "pre-fabricated" houses without the slightest bow in the direction of the farmers who pioneered it. But the farmers probably didn't care, their pride was in the building itself and not in the process that created it.

When the neighbors arrived for the Main Event, they were armed with their own pikes, forked poles from ten to thirty feet long. When the bent was

A Dutch barn adds pleasure to any valley view, such as this in Erie, Pennsylvania.

Some folks say that the Pennsylvania Dutch paint hex signs on their barns to protect them from evil spirits, but the farmers themselves have always maintained they are "chust for pretty."

moved into place, they used them to lift it into an upright position. It was done in stages with a respite between each lift, during which time the pikes were lowered one at a time to the next cross member in anticipation of the next upward push. The process was supervised and coordinated by post riders, who rode up with the bent at each cross member to make sure that the pikes had a good purchase on the wood and wouldn't slip, and also to make sure that all the pushing was done in unison. When the bent was in a full upright position they fastened ropes to hold it in place, and while some of the pike-wielding men on the floor below kept it

propped up, others went to work to raise a second bent at right angles to it. Once it was in place, they were lashed together with rope and some of the post riders went to work to brace them and pin them together with wooden pegs. When all of the sidewalls were in place, all hands went to work framing the rafters, and if everything went according to plan, the completely framed skeleton of the barn was solidly in place in time for dinner. By custom, the men who finished their assigned tasks first got first crack at the groaning board. It was a tactic that usually guaranteed that there wouldn't be any delays. The men were demons for hard work, but they did

In Pennsylvania's Berks County, few self-respecting farmers would be without hex signs on their barns, whatever the reason for putting them there might be. There is no denying that they are pretty, and evil spirits certainly stay clear of Berks County.

look forward to those monster picnics.

Obviously, there was still plenty of work to be done once the frame was in place. All any barn-raising produced was a skeleton. But that was the hard part and everyone involved knew that many hands make light work. The siding and roofing, which was far more time-consuming, but didn't require as much brawn, was left to the owner and his sons. But there were still plenty of willing hands in the neighborhood and men with free time to donate didn't mind offering help. There were usually plenty of leftovers to sweeten the deal, but more important was the prospect that the labor would be returned in kind whenever it was needed.

The job of building the barn usually began several seasons before the first tree was cut. The first steps were taken in the farmer's diary. Weather was all important and the plan had to take every possible change into account. A farmer had to know the path of the sun at different times of the year, where the prevailing winds blew and where to look for storms. He needed to know where the water went when it rained and where the snow drifted highest in the winter. The common wisdom was to slope the barn roof against the north wind, but the rule didn't hold true everywhere, and it was important for a farmer to know where the coldest blasts were likely to come from. Taking a drive in the country these days would suggest that most barns were built by the side of the road, but the barns were there first and the farm-to-market roads were most often laid out to be convenient to them, and not the other way around. Fortunately for the road builders, all the barns in a given area face the same way

A kitchen garden – one of the best things in life – in Bart, Pennsylvania.

A weatherbeaten Western classic in Montana.

and their challenge was simply to connect them.

That same drive in the country will produce images of an infinite variety of cupolas on barn roofs. The earliest barns didn't have them because ventilating holes were made in the gable ends and windows often went unglazed, but in the 18th century, farmers in Connecticut began expressing their individuality by putting one or two little turrets on the roofs of their barns. The idea spread to other parts of the country, not because farmers liked their decorative qualities but because they noticed that barns with cupolas were less likely to be struck by lightning. Every farmer knew that fresh hay in a barn created perfect conditions for a lightning strike, and it was easy for them to figure out that if the heat under the roof could be dissipated, then the electrical charge might go to the ground elsewhere. Of course, lightning rods had already been invented and it's a rare barn today that doesn't have them. But two hundred years ago, farmers who understood natural laws very well felt that grounded iron rods represented tampering with nature and they didn't want any part of them. Early advocates of lightning rods might as well have been talking to a stone wall when they told their neighbors how efficient they were. It was true that their barns were always left standing after a thunderstorm, but so were most that weren't protected, and their owners stubbornly refused to believe that an iron stick had anything to do with it. Then one day a lightning rod salesman who was also a marketing genius came up with an innovation that cast aside all the doubts. His rod was no better than any other, but at a point about half-way down from the top he had fastened a hollow glass ball. If lightning struck the rod, the glass broke and the farmer had visual evidence that without the rod his barn might be in ashes. There was no objection to the device after that, and when word got around there was hardly a barn anywhere without lightning rods. Better still, the people who sold them had a profitable sideline in replacing broken glass balls.

The practical Yankee farmers had long since been decorating the tops of their barns with weathervanes, to the delight of antique collectors today. But they didn't need to be sold on the idea. It was as important a piece of farm equipment as a good plow to men who could predict the weather by changes in wind direction with as much accuracy as a meteorologist today with a bank of computers. The first of them were made of lightweight wood that turned easily, but later generations who weren't opposed to decoration as their fathers had been began making them of metal and cast them in the shapes of such things as running horses and American eagles, but purists still contend that the only vane worth its salt is the one they started with, a simple piece of wood that can be turned by even a gentle breeze.

The roofs themselves have changed since the first days of settlement when most were sloped almost to the ground in a style New Englanders call a saltbox. In a generation or two, builders found it more practical to make gabled roofs with the sidewalls of the building forming the triangular roof line. It was modified in some places to become a hipped roof in which the building walls were all of uniform height and the roof sloped down from its ridge on all four sides. Both are still the most common, but dairy barns in

A Gothic masterpiece, South Livonia, New York.

particular have gambrel roofs, an innovation introduced to America about a hundred years ago, though it was commonly used in Europe for thousands of years before that. Like the gable, it ends at the sidewalls and defines their shape, but it rise up in two angles, one steep, ending at a ridge halfway up, and another gentler one continuing up to the peak, which allows more storage space for hay. Its name comes from a word that originally described the leg of a horse, and some historians theorize that the design evolved from a ridge pole that was inserted in farm buildings to hang sides of meat for curing. But it's just as likely that because of its jointed look the name would have been as appropriate if it had been developed as nothing more than a space-adding device. Whether it was created as a butcher's workroom or as a better hayloft, the gambrel roof has become a kind of icon in America. Whenever a building is intended to suggest a barn, whether it is a fast-food restaurant or a back yard storage shed, the connection is made with a gambrel roof, even though the majority of real barns in America don't have them.

Unfortunately, modern technology can't come close to building what most purists consider a "real" barn, which is one reason why the ones that are still standing should be considered genuine treasures. Until quite recent times, barns were built by the men who would use them and everything was done by hand. It all began with the cutting of trees, of course, but then the logs had to be hewn into square beams. The tool for that job was a broadax, a formidable piece of equipment that the farmer usually made himself before getting on with the job of building, and was as individual as the man himself. The work began with

A Dutch gambrel roof allows for plenty of storage space in a dairy barn.

A working farm on a Vermont hillside near West Barnet, and the solid stone barns of a Delaware estate seem to have little in common, but even if their form is different, their function is the same.

cutting notches in the log and then hacking out the space between them to turn the round surface into something flat. Sometimes finishing was done with an adze, a tool that resembles a heavy iron hoe, but just as often the heavy timbers were put into place with the scars of the broadax still on them. Over the years, the constant passing of sheaves over them smoothed them down and gave them a patina that can't be created any other way. To split the logs in two, they usually began the split with an iron wedge and then finished the job with wooden wedges and a sledgehammer. Though they preferred to do all the work themselves, even the earliest colonists sometimes patronized sawmills that

used water power to cut their logs into boards. The major crop of their fledgling farms was wood, and sawmill operators were usually willing to do the work in exchange for raw timber.

But the sawmill was the only commercial enterprise involved. A man's barn was his own creation and his special pride. He had traditional models for inspiration, but every inch of his barn was a personal statement. Using a straightedge and a square he worked long hours devising his plan, using interlocking squares and angles cut through them to create simple symmetry. It is a basic method architects use even today when they create building plans with computers, but the early

A full Pennsylvania tobacco barn has all its vents open to make use of every available breeze.

American farmers didn't know that. All they knew was that the square was basic to any good plan and that doors and windows as well as roof lines could easily be plotted by drawing diagonal lines through a square box or a series of them. The geometry of the interior, which in many barns is as inspirational as the interior of a cathedral, was accomplished in the same way. But without the aid of an architect or professional builders.

In our time, when farms are usually owned by conglomerates, the barns are models of efficiency, sometimes even to the point of including air conditioning units and piped-in music to keep the livestock happier and presumably more productive. Their humidity-controlled haylofts are loaded by huge machines and their threshing floors are like the service area of the big car dealership down the road where a pasture used to be. But here and there are still some barns that are reminders of a time when farms were rich and productive and the food they produced was, to borrow another newly-fashionable term,

"organic." They have a special beauty and the pride that went into them is still there adding a voice to the landscape that tells of a time when they sheltered fat cattle and housed the produce of the rich land; when they were home to cows that gave fresh milk through the same hands that cut the beams that supported the roof over their heads.

The mechanized farmer will say that many of them weren't planned carefully enough and that it was hard to get the chores done conveniently in most of the older barns. But his predecessors weren't in such a hurry. The chores got done, and at the end of a hard day a man could stand in the center of a great, cavernous structure he had built himself and look up at a mow two or three stories high filled to the rafters with sweet-smelling clover. He could look around him at well-fed, contented cattle bedded in clean straw up to their bellies. And if such a thing couldn't bring contentment to a man, why, probably nothing at all could.

The landmark star barn near Harrisburg, Pennsylvania.

Barns like this one in Ellensburg, Washington, are probably more appropriately called byres because their function is more for the shelter of animals than the storage of grain and fodder. The cupola helps provide ventilation, but in early barn designs that included louvers in the walls to allow air to pass through, cupolas were added to provide nesting places for pigeons, which farm families used for food and their oil for fuel.

When pioneers established farms and ranches in the West, they didn't have the luxury of an abundance of wood and stone to build elaborate barns. This forced their horses and other livestock to spend all of their time outdoors. The barns that early settlers did manage to build, like this one in Montana, are classic symbols of the Wild West, whose taming began when they became part of the landscape.

Variations on round barns are considered perfect for Wisconsin dairy farms.

Nearly all American barns have their origins in European designs, but the round barn is a product of pure Yankee ingenuity. The idea began in Massachusetts and spread quickly throughout New England – including Vermont where this one stands – and into the Midwest and Canada, where farmers found the shape more practical than the traditional rectangle that had been standard for centuries.

Very few of the earliest barns in America were ever painted. The idea of brightening their exteriors with a coat of paint began in Virginia, where the builder of this barn obviously decided not to follow the fashion. He did, however, bow to modern convenience by covering it with a tin roof, which will make the barn a cozy, if noisy, place to be when those dark clouds break.

What artist could ever ask for a better canvas than a barn door? They may never find their way to the Metropolitan Museum of Art, but the American countryside is covered with signs of life created by unknown artists who are generally quite good at painting what they see.

Although it dominates the scene, it takes more than a barn to make a farm.

A dovetail silo in Vermont. Above-ground silos didn't begin appearing on American farms until after the Civil War, when an Indiana farmer built one. He found that a round shape was best because it was easier to keep clean, but some farmers decided they were simpler to build as polygons with the sides dovetailed together. Some even made them square and others put them inside their barns, but over the years keeping them as separate structures and making them round has proven to be the best course.

A wooden silo, Pennsylvania. The engineering problem of constructing a round wooden tower was solved by most farmer-builders when they began raising vertical sidings and binding the boards together with metal hoops like a barrel. Dampness causes the wood to swell and makes the structure as watertight as the hull of a ship. Over time, wooden silos tend to lean at drunken angles and eventually need to be replaced, but their life expectancy is usually a good deal longer than that of the men who built them.

Ventilation holes add a decorative touch to a brick end Pennsylvanian barn.

We usually call tabbies house cats, but the lucky ones get to live in dairy barns where they have an important job to do standing guard against rodents. They are amply rewarded for their efforts with the richest diet of milk and cream a cat could possibly hope for.

A standard piece of equipment on a typical dairy barn is a weathervane, which stands guard on the roof to warn of sudden changes in the weather.

On Iowa farms, a windmill is as traditional as the barn itself.

Pristine symmetry, State College, Pennsylvania.

A fortress-like stone barn in Story City, Iowa.

Not every silo has a barn attached to it, and not every barn is attached to a silo. But even when they are separated from one another, it is a rare American farm that doesn't have both. And both take on a kind of serene beauty during the winter months, when they are protecting their contents from winter winds and snow.

A fascinating mixture of textures and color, Kutztown, Pennsylvania.

Grain elevators, bright before a blackening sky at Rexburg, Idaho.

Victims of progress, Altoona, Pennsylvania.

A gently sloping barn, ready for when the cows come home on a farm in Tennessee.

A barnyard without chickens and geese would be strangely quiet. But if they're not outside the barn, they are probably in it waiting to be fed. Ancient barns were conceived as enclosures around threshing floors for grain storage, but eventually space for animals was added along with living space for farm workers. It was usually a very orderly arrangement, with sleeping quarters for women above the stalls for cows and those for men above the stables. Pigs were relegated to the furthest end of the building and poultry were allowed to fend for themselves on the theory that they would always come home to roost.

An Ohio sixteen-sided barn. Modern barns come in a wide variety of sizes and shapes and if they don't house people any longer, their animal inhabitants still have their own assigned territories. The buildings themselves are as carefully built as the farmer's own house, with shingled roofs and glazed windows – luxuries undreamed of in the earliest barns.

The dowager queen of Wisconsin.

In an age of mechanized farming, when harvesting is often done from inside the air-conditioned cab of a giant tractor, some old barns still hold memories of a different era when oxen, horses and mules helped farmers get their job done. But romantic as the relics may be, they serve as reminders that life was far from easy in the good old days.

Tract houses fill the field behind this abandoned barn in Pennsylvania and some day in the near future they will probably replace it. But in the meantime, it stands as a memorial to the pride of the people who built and worked in it. The American landscape is filled with such monuments to our past, but, sadly, they are disappearing at an alarming rate.

A crisp dawn during the fall, when a barn is a warm and welcoming place.

When automobiles began appearing on country roads, itinerant barn painters offered free paint jobs to farmers who allowed them to add advertising messages to their work. Freestanding billboards ended the custom, but some farmers replaced ads for Bull Durham Tobacco with healthier messages of their own.

In some cases, the home-grown barn painters tend to get carried away with such devices as rainbows and cows wearing Pink Panther sunglasses, boots and bows. But the cows who call this Wisconsin barn home don't seem to mind, as long as no one tries to tie a red bow to their tails....

Some old barns serve as museums filled with oxcarts, surries and other antiques (above), but some are kept in repair because they are still the centerpieces of working farms in places like New York's Genesee Valley (right). The number of farms in the United States is slowly dropping, but there are still more than 2.17 million of them. On the other hand, average acreage is increasing, and Government estimates say that more than 991 million acres are currently being used for agriculture in the United States.

The idea of living in a log cabin has made a comeback in recent years, and although the modern versions come with dishwashers, storm windows and central heating, their owners find them quite rustic. There are few authentic log cabins left, but quite a few old log barns and, though they may seem humble to us, there is no place like them to the cows that call them home.

When great country estates began edging out farms in the Northeast, their owners were more interested in making a statement of affluence than imitating the practicality of their country cousins. This former stable in Spartenburg, Pennsylvania, though small, was its owner's idea of gentrified sophistication. His farmer neighbors may have found it a bit fussy, but his horses probably didn't mind.

Before they became part of the landscape, silos were built underground and old stone barns didn't have colorful towers to complement them.

In the early days of the West, cattle barns followed more traditional lines before cowpunchers discovered the practicality of the round barn.

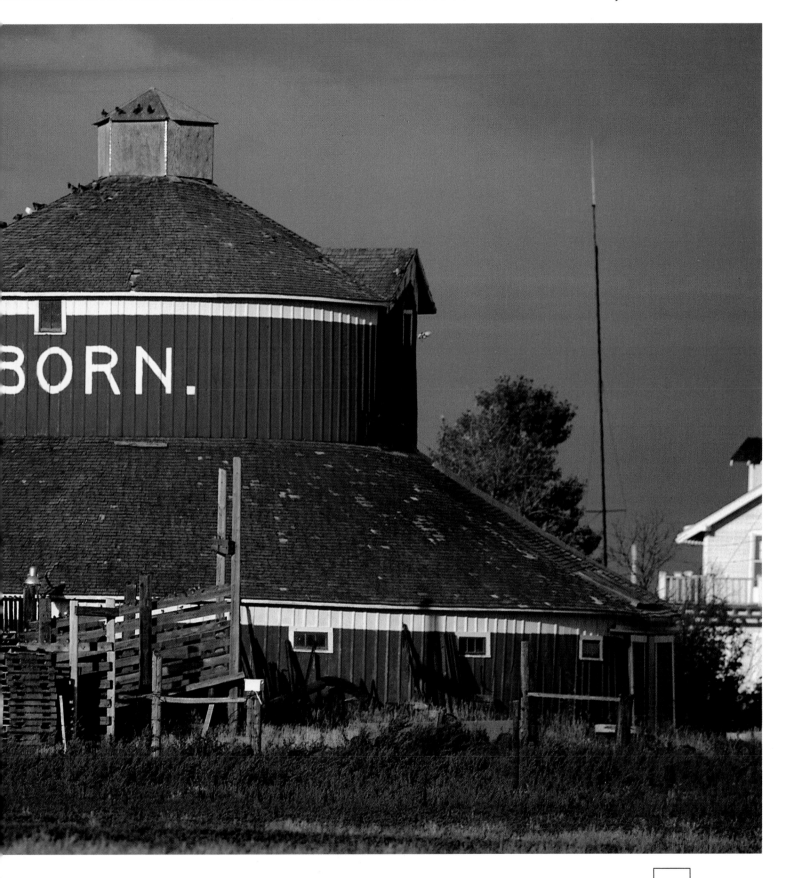

The sign on the side of an old octagonal barn is a plea to save the farm. But anyone who takes on the job is going to have his work cut out for him. The same problems are presented by a grand old round barn in Wisconsin on which age has taken its toll from the foundation to the top of the roof. Historic preservation, it seems, is a movement too often confined to cities.

A grande dame in Greene, New York.

There is a museum-like quality to the farms of the Amish in Pennsylvania, but they are not dusty reminders of the past. Work goes on there just as it did a century ago, and probably a century from now they'll still be thriving in the same old way.

At first glance, this barn in Pullman in Washington looks like a covered
haystack, which may well have been the inspiration for its design. It is a
rare barn anywhere that isn't a triumph of simple design and an affirmation
of the architectural dictate that form should follow function.

A new lease of life for a barn in Media, Pennsylvania.

Art imitates nature in the mountains of Oregon. Barns are nearly always built with one eye on prevailing weather conditions and the other on terrain. Very few farmers have ever taken aesthetics into account in siting their barns, but most have succeeded quite well in enhancing the beauty of the natural landscape.

The owners of this 1899 barn in Passumpsic, Vermont, say it is the first ever built in a circular shape. In fact, the first was built by Massachusetts Shakers nearly seventy-five years earlier, but this may well be the first made of wood, which presented its builders with a problem not faced by the Shakers, whose creation was in stone.

Barn design is often compared to that of churches, and this one in Pennsylvania makes the comparison seem obvious.

Not every barn follows traditional lines. The 347-foot McKinney Block Barn in Cuba, New York, might well be a factory.

This tobacco barn hasn't changed since it was part of colonial Pennsylvania.

A little farm huddles round its barn in Homer City, Pennsylvania, dwarfed by the cooling towers of a huge nuclear power plant.

The granddaddy of all round barns, the beautiful Wedgewood blue and white stone barn in the Hancock Shaker Village, Massachusetts.

A church that was originally a barn in Mannington, West Virginia.

In places where winters are fierce, such as New England, barns are often attached to farmhouses, a feature that makes life easier for farmers as the chores have to be done whatever the weather.